Writer, the World Needs You

Get Past Your Fear and Write the Words You're Meant to Write

Alix Moore

Rising Moon Press
Clarksburg, Maryland

Rising Moon Press
24110 Clarksburg Road
Clarksburg, MD 20871
http://www.writerswithwings.com/

Book Layout © 2014 BookDesignTemplates.com
Cover by Creative Medium, Ltd.
Writer, the World Needs You/Alix Moore
ISBN: 978-0692415696

For Karen,
for Jack,
for all the writers of the weekly meditation group:
This book is your fault.

This book is also for you, Writer:
to encourage you to look within
to find the words your spirit demands you write,
and to help you find the courage you need
to face the fear your creative journey brings.

CONTENTS

Four a.m.

It's four a.m., and the voice of this book is clear in my head.

I admit, it took some persuading to pull myself out of the nest of my bed, with my partner breathing beside me, and the dog breathing from the floor, and the whole soft space perfectly conformed to my body and my comfort. But here I am, with a fresh cup of coffee, and the lights on.

Because the words came. And they're for you.

This whole book is for you, Writer.

Part One:

Introduction

Writer, claim the name!

If you have ever filled a notebook
    Or a computer screen
    Or even the space inside your head
    With words that came from somewhere
    Inside or beyond you
    Words that teased
    Flirted
    Coaxed
    Words that couldn't be stopped

    If you have known
    The inexorable call of Muse
    In the middle of the night
    In the middle of the road
    In the middle of something else you were really supposed
    To be doing
    And if you yielded to that call
    And let the words come
    (And the consequences be damned)
    Then there is no doubt:
    You are of the tribe.
    You write.

You, Writer.

It doesn't matter if you have never published, or even shared, your work.

It doesn't matter if it's only you who thinks it's good—or if you think it's terrible.

Judgment and praise are just two sides of the validation coin. (We'll talk about that later.)

You are a writer because you write.

Say it:

I am a writer.

Practice introducing yourself:

Hi, I'm Alix. I'm a writer.

And if that fearbelly thing happens, we'll get to that later, too. I promise. Actually, it's unavoidable. Creativity carries the baggage of fear.

(Until you learn to set it down.)

Earth needs the wisdom of all her children.

I'm writing this book because I have been reading. I have immersed myself in books of advice for writers. Advice about how to get readers to read your books. Advice about how to become visible, to build a platform and market yourself, how to find or make purple cows and Twitter friends.

And all these books have some truth and some value (for me). But I know that your writer's journey begins long before you're ready to market. **Platform building is important, but it's not the beginning, and the beginning is what I want to talk to you about.**

It's not important that you share my spiritual viewpoint (and I promise I won't let it get in the way too often). It *is* important that you write, however, and that you share your work with the world.

You are here on this planet at this time for a reason, and your marvelous creativity is no coincidence. There are words only you can write, messages only you can carry.

But I know that your vision of yourself might need a little fine-tuning—that you might need some help seeing clearly what your mission is.

And I know that there's a fear factor to contend with—that you have been programmed with messages of caution, with a legacy of fear. So, to get to the writing you were born to do, you need to tune in, trust yourself, and cope with the fear-dust that gets kicked up along the way.

I've walked that path. I can help you with that. Will you let me?

Earth needs the wisdom of all her children.

First of all, not everything you read in this book will be true.

Don't believe what I say unless it resonates with you.

Unless it makes your head nod, your heart leap, goose bumps rise, your stomach clench in fear. (We'll get to the fear in a bit.)

Unless it *feels* and *sounds* and *tastes* like truth. Your truth. And you will know if it does. Listen to your heart and your belly. Trust yourself.

And it's likely that some parts will be true (for you) and others won't. And that's fine.

So, are you ready to get started? Here's the first important question: **Why should anyone read what you write?**

Part Two: Finding the Words You Were Meant to Write

Why should anyone read what you write?

It's a marketing question, a branding question, a soul question.

What light are you here to carry?

What words do you hold?

What are you bringing to the party of the planet, right now, this minute? What story will, except for you, go untold?

And how much is the fear stopping you?

We all carry fear. Creativity is married to shame.

Consider that mix of joy and mud as an invitation.

An invitation to follow the pull of the god/dess in your veins, to let the words write you until you are full of grace, until you are healed, until the only voices in your head are those of love and gratitude for this godself called you.

Are you still with me? Or has the fear won?

Humanity has suckled on shame. Fear has driven us, real as stones, out of our power and our lives. But that time is gone. This lifetime, we are asked to stand as light, bright in the power we are, knowing the value of the gift of our lives. But I digress. (Sort of.) You don't have to walk in my spiritual truth to follow me in this conversation about you, the writer.

The bottom line is: Marketing doesn't matter. Money doesn't matter. Reviews and TV shows and interviews and household name recognition: All these will come when they're ready, although rarely if you chase them. But they're not what matters most. (Or if they are, you're reading the wrong book!)

What matters most is that you touch the heart of what you are here to give, and that you wade through the fear until you are able to deliver your words to the world. Until you can answer the second important question:

How is your art meant to be in service to your readers, and to the planet?

Just to reassure you: Being in service does not mean that you should give your work away for free. To keep the scales balanced, what is received must equal what is given. Gifts flow back as they are given. So don't worry—if you find the courage to serve your readers, the money will come.

But what *are* your gifts? What are the words you are meant to write?

What do you bring to the party?

The planet is one giant block party. The music is loud, the (non-alcoholic) drinks are cold, and we are all invited to dance in the street.

But nobody shows up empty-handed to a block party. Each neighbor brings his or her specialty, and it's the same with artists and writers.

You may already know what you are here to offer, in which case you may not need this section of the book. But for the rest of you, finding your purpose and your passion might take some time and some consideration. It took me about ten years of questioning to sort out that answer for myself. I'm hoping to help you get there a little faster than that!

Here's an exercise that might help.

(Grab a blank piece of paper, and some markers, a pencil, or paint.)

The core of you

In the center of your paper, draw yourself, either as a person or as an image that represents you. Perhaps you see yourself as a tree or a kite or a bridge.

(Many of us have metaphors of self that flow with us through the years. If this kind of thinking is new to you, just pick something and go with it. You can always revise it.)

Your hats, your passions, your gifts

Around the outside of the image of yourself that you have just drawn, I want you to place some more images—words and pictures that capture the bright facets of you. Where do you shine? What do you love? Where have you found success or touched the lives of others?

What talents do you have that could benefit your readers?

This is a question to ponder, to take with you on long walks, or to dream about during a long commute. Drawing pictures and making lists is just a means to an end—a way to turn your conscious and unconscious attention to this important question.

So allow yourself to think outside the box, to create and revise as many times as you need to. Release judgment and don't worry when fear pops up. Be playful.

Here is my diagram, as I drew it a few years ago in my quest to understand the gifts I carry.

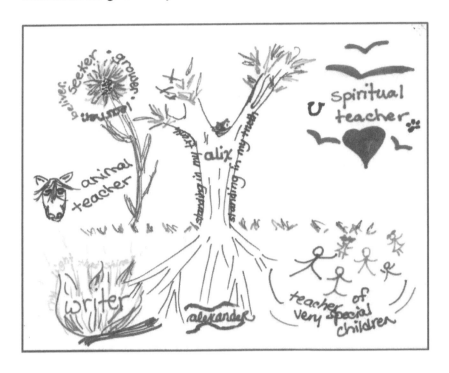

Start asking the question: What am I here to do? How am I supposed to serve?

At this time in my life, I consider myself a writer, a spiritual teacher, and an inspirational speaker. I didn't always know that about myself, however. I started the process of discovery, oddly enough, with Amway.

I was in my late thirties and working as a teacher when it became clear to me that I would never be able to afford to retire from teaching. So I started looking around for an additional stream of income. Through a friend of a friend, I got involved in Amway (called Quixtar at that time).

Amway and I were a terrible match, but I learned two things that were invaluable. I learned that I could dream, and that I had the power to make my dreams come true. I also got exposed to the world of business books.

I was very influenced by Robert G. Allen's book *Multiple Streams of Income*, and by Shad Helmstetter's *Who Are You Really and What Do You Want?*

As I devoured the Amway motivational recordings and read dozens of business books, I became more and more convinced that I had talents that I could share with the world and that those talents could support me financially. I just didn't know exactly what talents I was talking about!

So I just lived with the question. For years. I kept asking: *What can I do? What am I here to offer?* And more recently, *How can I serve?*

Questions are powerful. When we live with a question, the truth of the answer reveals itself bit by bit; it's as if you are peeling the layers of an onion until you reach the small green shoot in the center.

So will it take you years to figure out your own gifts? It might, but it doesn't matter. You can get started sharing them, anyway, and they and you can grow and change over time.

Which brings us back to the writing. Since you are reading this book, I am making the logical assumption that writing is one of your passions, one of the things that lights your lights. You just might need a little help fine-tuning the kind of writing you are driven to do. You might need help defining your gift.

So let me ask you a few more questions, and let's see where we end up.

If you weren't afraid, what would you write?

Sonia Choquette taught me to ask the "If you weren't afraid" question. It's a great one, and it often cuts to the heart of the mission, helping us see clearly through the fog of the fear.

You can ask this question in meditation, you can ask it out loud with one hand on your heart, you can ask it in writing and see what answer comes. Just say, "If I weren't afraid" and finish the sentence. Just let the words pop out—don't overthink it.

Each of us has stories that we are afraid to tell. My first published book was such a story. I was working on a completely different manuscript when along came *Tapping the Well Within.* That book demanded to be written, to be published, and required me to step out of the spiritual closet in a big way to share it with the world.

Because of that book, I had to admit I believe in fairies. Sorry, guys, but that's a hard one. Much more socially acceptable to have a guardian angel.

And not only did I have to write about fairies and spirit guides and the whole clairvoyant world within, I had to then stand up and *talk* about it. *In front of people.*

It took me years to have the courage to speak the truth of that book, and often I find I still censor myself. The god words still just don't want to come out of my mouth. But I'm working on it.

The thing about fear—each of us has our own kind of fear.

I'm not at all afraid of breaking the rules or speaking in public, and you might be. Although the specifics change, the fear factor is universal. And it's one of the things we, as writers, are asked to face, to face down.

And it's one of my reasons for being here—to work through my own fear, and to support you as you work through yours. If you'll let me.

What if you weren't worried about what your readers want?

How many times have you heard the advice to write what the readers want? A lot? I just finished reading a great little book about marketing, written by a very successful author, whose entire career is driven by creating and delivering what his readers want.

But I'm asking you to do something completely different. Different, more challenging, and way more exhilarating.

I'm asking you to be driven by *what your spirit wants*.

I am inviting you to write the deepest truth you have, the one that coils in the center of your belly, the one you can barely stand to peek at, with your head under the covers for fear of it.

I am asking you to hear your soul truth. I am asking you to write your light. I am asking you to write the message you are here to deliver and then . . . and then I'm going to ask you to share it with the world.

What you write from your soul will always find readers.

(Whew! A little *woo woo* there, perhaps. But the world needs *woo woo*. In fact, *woo* is the new black. But I digress. Again.)

What about the fiction writers?

So, if you are a writer who writes nonfiction self-help books, then it's pretty easy to see what you are here to bring to the planet. (Although, even then, it may not be quite what you think it is!)

But what about those many folks who write fiction, who write to entertain us? It's true that some writers write to be read for pleasure, but that's not the end of the conversation. You may have written a mystery, but there is a whole world wrapped around the story you are telling. You have thousands of words to share with your reader, and their impact can go way beyond the genre of your book.

What is the world view that is woven throughout your words? What truths do you promulgate? Even in a work of fiction, authors are creating meaning and purpose; they are teaching. In a work of fiction, the author's truth can be powerfully conveyed, since the readers' emotions are enlisted along with their imagination, to allow them to submerge their awareness completely into the world of the book.

But what kind of world are we choosing to inhabit for the hours that we read? What kind of world are we choosing to create when we write? It matters.

With a little reflection, you can find the core truths woven through your fiction. Then you might consider what truths you would embed if you wrote the stories you are afraid to write. Don't judge yourself, but bring awareness like a bright light into the creative space you inhabit. Know what you do—and why you do it. And then, when the fear hits, as it will, you can sustain yourself with your sense of purpose. You will be motivated to deal with dirt.

Part Three: Dealing with Your Fearbelly

As you move forward on your creative path, there will be hundreds of moments of fear.

This fear will come in small doses—and huge ones. It will masquerade as anxiety, procrastination, and lack of technological expertise. You will hear the fear in the voices inside your head, telling you that what you have to share is valueless. You will wade through the fear in the moments when the learning curve appears insurmountable. You may find yourself paralyzed with fear and completely unable to move forward. (And then you might beat yourself up for your procrastination. But it's really just the fear factor.)

I want to talk frankly about fear, because it's the elephant in the room—the reality that many writing books just don't talk about. (Kudos to Jeff Goins and Tim Grahl for tackling this important topic.) And I want to go one step further, to show you that the fear is an essential part of your life journey. It illuminates the places that we need to heal, and motivates us to grow.

Let's start with the voices inside your head. When a writer is immersed in the creative flow, she is a goddess. The words just come, and for those moments of creation, the judgment stops. But before and after flow, the voices inside our heads are loud, and they tell us to doubt ourselves.

Sometimes our inner conversation comes in a recognizable personality. We might hear the voice of a judgmental teacher or that of a parent who, in trying to keep us safe, inadvertently conveyed the message that we weren't good enough. Sometimes the voices are just there, and although our mind does not believe them, our belly does. Our fearbelly does.

It's helpful to think of that roiling pit of panic that slows us down, or prevents us from even starting out, as an entity complete unto itself. I call it the fearbelly, and it is not susceptible to logic.

If you are going to move forward with your creative voice, in a state of confidence and grace, you will have to address the belly beast, and learn to feed it truth until even your bones know what you are worth.

We write in order to heal the fear.

We publish in order to heal the fear.

We market (yikes!) because we need to heal the fear.

Fear is not the obstacle to the journey; it* is *the journey.

I've heard the phrase "fear of success" all my life. I don't really think that we are afraid of success or failure, per se, but I do believe that many of us are afraid to be visible, to expose the pale underbellies of our souls to the scorn and judgment of others. It's a real fear, and a powerful problem, since the outside world is full of those who will throw dirt. And often, the more we stand in our truth and shine in our own light, the more we will be attacked. And sometimes the brightest among us are assassinated; so the threat is real.

The more that our creative work is connected to the core purpose of our lives, the harder all these things are.

If we are writing about and sharing something that is peripheral to our core purpose, then the fear is less intense.

So look for the place of utmost terror, and there it is: the treasure of your growth, the place to be healed, the untrue truth you have been carrying and long to set down.

It is through healing the fear that we heal ourselves and can then courageously share our words and our art with the world, thereby contributing our necessary measure to the healing of the collective.

The good news is: You don't have to do it all at once. You can nibble on the edges of the fear cookie, until one day you glance at it and there are nothing but crumbs of terror, easily brushed off.

I know this truth. I have walked this journey in hundreds of ways over dozens of years and thousands of lifetimes. I know we are here to be our bright divine selves. And I want you to know it, as well.

What do I want you to know? I want you to know

That you are human and also divine

That the fear has a purpose

That it doesn't have to win

That facing it can make you immeasurably stronger

That this is the lifetime where everything shifts

That opening to your words and sending them forth is a sacred calling, no matter what it is you think you write.

And if my words can help in any way as you wade through the swamp, if I can support you as you find the courage to shine, then all is well and I am on purpose.

Common Fears

It's not enough to know you are afraid. You must ask the question, "Afraid of what?"

When we attempt to resolve fear in a general way, it's an almost unsurmountable task. If a client of mine realizes that fear is the reason she is experiencing writer's block, that's an important insight and the first step to coping with the fear. That client needs to dig down, however, until she can see more clearly what thing or things she is worried about. Is it fear of being judged by reviewers, friends, or family? Is she speaking a truth that is going to make her readers uncomfortable? Is she likely to get pushback, or hate mail, from her readers? Does social media feel like a confusing necessity that will be an invasion of her privacy?

Each of these underlying causes of fear might require a different solution. When we are clear about the exact nature of our fear, then we are simultaneously clear about the exact nature of our healing. But what about that healing? How do we move through and past the fear? How do we stand in confidence and joy as we bring our gift of words to the world?

The problem is, most of us were never taught effective ways to cope with fear, and so when we face it or when we find ourselves mired in the swamp of growth, we have no tools to help us. Some of us turn to therapy, and others turn to substance abuse, but really, all we need are some strategies—a toolbox for dealing with fear.

I'm going to share with you a bunch of tools that have helped me work through the fear moments. But first, let's talk about some of the common kinds of fear you might face in your writer's life.

Technology terrors

Oddly enough, most writers I know, myself included, can be really stuck in the swamp of anxiety and frustration when faced with the many technological challenges that today's writers must master. For young writers, just getting out of school, this is perhaps less of an issue. But for those of us who are fifty-plus, and coming to writing as a second career or at least a serious hobby, then coping with all of the Internet- and computer-related writing tasks can be a serious road block.

I remember when I was just starting out, how much I wanted to hand it all over—all the website challenges and marketing plans. I just wanted to pay someone to do it for me! But of course, since I wasn't yet successful, I couldn't afford to do so.

And I think that's where many writers stand. With limited budgets, we are forced to dig in and figure things out. There are so many details to figure out! And when you mix anxiety about becoming more visible with technology that's out of your comfort zone, then you have a potent recipe for procrastination.

So if you are feeling stymied or overwhelmed by something you need to learn that involves a computer, know this: That learning is part of the journey. As we face each little challenge and pull ourselves up by the bootstraps, we grow in confidence, which stands us in good stead when our work is finally ready to go public. So tell yourself that you can do it, and put on your Feisty Writer hat. (That's in your courage toolbox; so read on.)

Fear of technology is really the fear that we don't have what it takes to get the job done—the fear that we aren't good enough.

Fear of judgment: the voices inside your head

Everyone carries critical voices inside their heads.

The voices that tell us we aren't smart enough, thin enough, good enough.

Voices that come from the media, our parents, our teachers—even our past lives.

Voices that we have internalized until they speak with our own voice, telling us the myriad ways in which we don't measure up.

The voices inside our heads make proclamations; they tell us what isn't true with such conviction that we believe it *is* true—and immutable.

I'm fat!

I'm always late for everything.

My friends will think I'm crazy.

I don't have a big enough platform. I'll never get an agent.

Everyone knows you can't make money as a writer.

You know what your internal voices are telling you, and you may recognize whose voice they are speaking in.

These critical voices are especially challenging for writers because criticism and judgment shut down creativity. They are one possible reason for the state of noncreating we call writer's block.

Judgment works in two directions, however. When we judge other writers, when we judge anyone, it gives power to that part of us that judges ourselves. So if you would like to stop judging yourself, one place to start is by making a commitment to stop judging others.

You can use mirror work and bubbles from your courage toolbox to help with the voices and the judgment of others.

The critical voices inside our head are trying to keep us small. When we grow strong enough to disregard them, then we are strong enough to stand in our truth and shine.

Fear of being seen

The fear of speaking to a group is very common and completely logical. When we stand up and address an audience, we make ourselves visible. We are there, in front of the group, where anyone can throw dirt at us. Part of the fear of speaking up, whether at a critique group, a book signing, or an open mic, is that fear of being seen—and of being judged or ridiculed or somehow found to be less than good enough.

But there's another layer of vulnerability when we speak or read about our deepest truths. You might be able to speak to a group as your business self and yet be terrified to read your own words at an open mic event. That's because our soul truth matters, at a very deep level, and it challenges our confidence accordingly.

If you find yourself traumatized by the thought of sharing your words in front of a group, try taking little baby steps. Speak first to the most supportive group you can imagine, and move on from there. You might consider Toastmasters, or start by sharing recordings of yourself in podcasts on a blog or via iTunes.

This fear of being seen extends beyond public speaking, however, and can include anxiety about using social media and even reluctance to publish and promote your books.

It might help you to know that your soul remembers lifetimes when speaking out and standing fully in your power and light resulted in death. (Think of witch hunts—wouldn't that be enough to give you stage fright?) Although it can happen, you're not as likely to die in this lifetime from speaking out, but your memories don't know that!

Fear of being seen is often the fear of death.

Fear by any other name

Before we move on to tools for dealing with fear, I just want to remind you of all of the masks that fear can wear. I use the single word "fear" in this book, partly for simplicity's sake and partly because it's accurate. But you might recognize your personal fear in one of these words:

- Anxiety (free-floating or focused)
- Insecurity
- Self-doubt
- Low self-esteem
- Negative self-talk
- Procrastination
- Envy
- Jealousy
- Judgment
- Perfectionism
- Feeling overwhelmed
- Powerlessness

- Lack of follow-through
- Stress (no time to write!)

What mask does *your* fear like to hide behind?

Cleaning up the fear

So enough about why we are scared—let's do something about the fear!

Dealing with fear is easier fear if you

- Know that it's there, for everyone (although each person's fear wears different clothing)
- Know that it's rarely logical
- Bite off teeny-tiny teensy-weensy chunks of challenge—just take a baby step into what scares you
- Forgive yourself (stop judging yourself!)
- Let it take the time it takes—after all, you have a lifetime!

One of the best ways to move past your fear is to have a toolbox of courage tools. In the next section, you will find some of my favorites, in no particular order.

A Hint: If these tools are new to you, then I suggest you read through them once and then choose one tool, the one that resonates most with you, and practice it over several days or weeks. When you feel comfortable, add another courage tool to your toolbox. Over time, you will develop a repertoire of fear-busting strategies.

Hint #2: These tools only work if you actually practice them! Just reading about them is not enough.

Part Four: Your Courage Toolbox

Get grounded

I have been a writer all my life; yet when I learned to meditate, it changed my creative process completely. No longer at the mercy of the Muse, I could meet her anytime in the deep connection with my own spirit that I found in the meditation space.

Not only is meditation a powerful gateway to creativity; it's a powerful way to release fear and allow insights to surface.

I practice a simple, grounding meditation. Here's how to do it.

Sit in a comfortable seat with your feet flat on the floor. Close your eyes.

With your imagination, pick a color of light, and attach a tube of light in that color to the base of your spine.

Let the tube of light extend down through your body, through your chair, and down through the building that you are in, until it reaches the center of the earth. Attach the tube of light securely to the center of the earth.

Allow the tube of light to expand until it is as big around as your physical body. It should be as wide at the bottom as it is at the top. This tube of light is called a grounding cord, and it connects you with the planet.

On the tube of light there is a release switch. Turn it on, and allow all the energy that no longer serves you to flow down the grounding cord (your light tube) until it reaches the center of the earth, where it can be recycled.

Let go of the past, of fear, of struggle, rejection, or failure. Let go of the energy other people have left in your space and the energy of unhealthful food you have eaten or unethical things you have done.

You don't need to identify the energy you are releasing, just set your intention to clear out anything that it's not in your best interest to carry. Release anything that is blocking your path.

Sit like this for ten to twenty minutes, or as long as you like. Don't worry about anything your mind does during this time. It doesn't matter.

When you are finished meditating, always end with the golden sun activity (see the next page), to leave your newly cleaned space full of good energy.

If you come back to this meditation space at another time, simply release the old grounding cord and let it fall down into the center of the earth before you choose a new one.

Please note: The goal of this meditation is not to quiet your mind, although that will eventually happen. I know many people with active minds who really want and need to practice meditation, yet who give up because they can't force their minds to be still. Don't worry about it!

If you feel distracted or fidgety during your meditation time, try these solutions:

- Set a timer for ten to fifteen minutes and sit with your eyes closed until the time is up, no matter what your mind is doing.
- Play meditation music (I love the "Calm Meditation" channel on Pandora.com!).
- Use the "blow bubbles" tool from this toolbox and just keep dumping your fidgets into bubbles.

You will find a growing collection of recorded meditations for writers on my website, writerswithwings.com.

Golden sun

The golden sun exercise is a powerful way to fill yourself up with courage or patience or any good energy you choose. Use the exercise after meditation or after a session of bubbles—or anytime you just want more positive energy in your space.

Take a moment to sit or stand, with your feet flat on the floor and your eyes closed.

Imagine a huge golden sun above your head. Fill this sun full of any energy that you would like more of in your space: effortless creativity, courage, time to write—whatever you choose.

Pop the sun and allow the energy inside to flow down through the top of your head. Let some of it run across your shoulders, down your arms, and out your hands. Let the rest of it flow down through your body and out your feet until it surrounds you on the outside, as well as filling you on the inside.

Sit for a few moments in the glow, until you are ready to open your eyes and move on.

Blow bubbles

Bubbles are a powerful way to visualize and clear unwanted energy from your space. This technique works best if you are meditating (see the "get grounded" tool, above), but you can use bubbles on their own, any time when you can sit or stand for a moment with your eyes shut—so not while driving unless you are in the passenger seat!

With your feet flat on the floor and your eyes closed, imagine a huge shimmering bubble out in front of you. It can be any color that you want.

Begin to dump fear into the bubble. See it flowing out of you and filling up the bubble in front of you. You can also dump impatience, envy, frustration, rejection, or any negative emotion that you want.

Fill up the bubble until it can't hold any more, then send it off to the edge of the universe and blow it up. Don't forget this step—it doesn't do much good to fill up bubbles and leave them hanging around in your energy space!

Get another bubble, and repeat the whole procedure until you send the last one off.

This is a powerful practice for dealing with any kind of anxiety or fear, and you can do it over and over, as often as you need to. So next time you are stewing over something, take action! Blow the negative energy out of your space, using bubbles. (Then go for a walk!)

After you've moved out negative energy with bubbles, it's a good idea to refill your energy space with positive energy, using the golden sun visualization, just as you do at the end of a meditation.

Go for a walk

Being outside in nature is a powerful healing and grounding force. Going for a walk in the woods is a great thing to do when you feel stuck in fear. The act of walking, of being outdoors, helps you quiet your mind. It allows your attention to settle in your body, and the physical exercise clears and renews your body.

Do

- Take the dog if you have one.
- Leave the cell phone in your pocket.
- Leave the music behind—be mostly silent.
- Walk alone or with a quiet companion.
- Choose a wooded trail instead of a city block.
- Pay attention to the sights and sounds and smells around you.
- Let your mind wander.
- Allow the walk to be what it is, with no judgment or expectation.
- Consider bringing along a voice recorder or a small notebook for the words that might float up.
- Breathe!

Egg magic

We all have a tendency to spend our energy outside of ourselves. Whenever we focus our attention at work, worry about world issues or family members, or daydream about the future or the past, we send streamers of our energy out of ourselves to those people and places.

Most of us also unwittingly allow other people's energy inside our core space. If you have ever spent time with a person who makes you feel either refreshed or drained, you have experienced this energy exchange.

We don't want other people inside our core space, however, since that lets us experience their emotions and their opinions of us at a visceral level.

I'm not saying that we shouldn't love and be intimate, just that we don't need anyone but ourselves inside our personal energy fields. (Do you really want to submerge yourself into your loved one, without boundaries, or do you want to be fully yourself, in love?)

Clear energy boundaries are especially important for artists and writers, who can touch so many lives with their creativity. The clearer our energy fields are, the easier it is to tap into our creative wisdom. The voice of our higher selves needs silence to be heard.

So we need a tool that keeps us inside our energy boundaries—and keeps other people out. My young students dubbed this tool "egg magic."

All people have the ability to work with their energy in this and other meditations. Depending on your level of experience, you may see, imagine, or simply intend the following exercise:

Sit in a comfortable seat with your feet flat on the floor. Take one deep, opening breath. Close your eyes and inhale through your nose. Pause, and then exhale through your mouth. Then spend a moment just breathing normally and deepening your connection to Earth. When you are ready, become aware of your aura. Your aura is the energy field that wraps around your physical body. As you sit and breathe quietly, picture your aura shifting until it fills up the space from your physical body outward, to just past your fingertips. You may need to call it back from far away, or allow it to expand from close up against you.

When you have settled your aura around you, look for all the places where your energy is sending out fingers and strings to connect with others. Even with those you love, your energy belongs in your space, not theirs!

Imagine a magnet at your center, calling to all those streamers of energy. Pull yourself back inside of you. See more and more bits of you coming back home, inside your aura space. Like an egg, you are luminous and bounded. The more energy you call back, the more brightly you will glow.

Feel the safety of the egg of you: spirit inside of body, body inside of aura, aura with outer limits that say, "I stop here." Imagine graffiti painted on the outside of your egg that tells other people, "You stop here!"

Sit in the peace of your clear boundaries until you are ready to stop. Finish, as always, with a golden sun visualization.

This energy that you have gathered in is now yours to do with as you choose, whether you choose to garden, to paint, or to nap.

Take baby steps

Those of us with a passion tend to put our eyes on the goal; we can see where we are going, and we're impatient to get there. This impatience can leave us feeling frustrated that everything is taking soooo long! Often we criticize ourselves for our slow rate of progress.

But growth takes the time it takes. If you are tackling a core life mission, then there are lots of fears and false truths to wade through. It's like playing that old game of Mother May I? You can occasionally take a giant leap forward, but mostly you just take lots of baby steps.

And baby steps are a great way to cope with fear. When thinking of something you know you need to do, something that seems overwhelming and scary, then consider that thing your goal. And then ask yourself, "What's one little thing I can do today that moves me in that direction?"

Growth takes the time it takes.

For example, if you think you need a large social media presence for your writing, but the idea of it feels like an intolerable invasion of your privacy, consider starting with some research: How do Facebook, Twitter, and Google+ differ? What about LinkedIn and Pinterest? Which one is the best fit for you and your creative work?

Gathering information is a reasonable first step. Then, for example, consider joining Facebook, putting up a minimal profile, and spending some time exploring its professional pages and groups.

When you give yourself permission to take just one teensy-weensy step in the direction of your goal, then the fear—and the learning curve—becomes manageable.

Just make sure to turn off the critical voices inside your head that tell you you're not moving fast enough! Remember, it can take twenty years to become an overnight success.

Put on your Feisty Writer hat

Many years ago, I moved to a small farm. Although I had worked with horses for years, I had always lived in the city or the suburbs. Life in the country was new, wonderful, and challenging!

I had to learn to run a chainsaw, to fix my own plumbing, to deal with the occasional live snake or dead groundhog. Even riding the tractor took courage—it was a big tractor!

In those first years, there were so many things I didn't know how to do and felt a little afraid of trying. But I was determined! I had a sun visor custom embroidered, with the words "Feisty Bitch" written across the front of it.

Whenever I had to gear up for a new challenge, I got out my feisty hat, literally, and wore it as I tackled the project. It may sound silly, but the hat really helped me be courageous.

So consider creating a Feisty Writer hat for yourself—a literal hat or some other talisman that reminds you that yes, you *can* do it!

Practice acceptance and allowing

How's your self-talk these days?

Are you your own worst critic?

We all carry such judgmental voices inside our heads. We tell ourselves we aren't doing it right, we're too slow, or we aren't good enough.

A good antidote to this self-judgment is the practice of allowing.

Allow yourself to be where you are, to take the time you need, to walk your path whatever way you are walking it.

When you sit down to write, set the clear intention that whatever happens with your work is what is meant to be at that moment. If you really can't write and decide to spring-clean your house, accept it. If you are supposed to be working on Project A, but your heart is singing with Project B, go for it.

Go with the flow.

Release the need to be in charge, to push, to make things happen.

Let the path walk you.

Trust yourself.

Breathe.

Know that all is well in your world.

Mirror work

I learned about mirror work from Louise Hay. It's very powerful. Simple, yet challenging to do.

Mirror work consists of looking at yourself in a mirror and speaking a message of love to yourself. It can be as simple as

Alix, I love you.

Or as specific as

Alix, you are a fabulous writer, and the world needs your words.

Look yourself in the eye and speak your message of love. Try it every day for forty days, and see what it does to your fearbelly.

The opposite of fear is love.

Go on a validation diet

Dr. Wayne Dyer often talks about the importance of "striving to be independent of the good opinion of others."

It's a powerful concept that leads to the realization that praise and criticism are two sides of the same coin. When we accept the praise of others and allow it to inflate our sense of self-worth, then inevitably we also remain vulnerable to the criticism of others.

Metaphysical feminist Christine Agro invites us to accept praise as an acknowledgment of our own worth, not as a validation of it.

If I praise you for being a good writer, and you *know* you are a good writer, then my praise holds little power over you. If I praise your good writing, however, and you are not really sure how good you are, then my words might fill up a small empty space of doubt within you. If my praise makes you feel better, then my criticism can make you feel worse. And that leads to a roller coaster of emotion in which other people's opinions about and reviews of your work either make or ruin your day.

The ground remains far steadier beneath your feet when you know the work you are here to do, when you know the value that your work brings to your readers, when you know that your job is to stand in your own light and your own truth, no matter who throws dirt at you.

It's one thing to know in your head that you need to be independent of the opinions of others, but it's something else again to embody that knowledge, to be truly secure and confident in your own light. That takes work and commitment and practice. Remembering your purpose will help you embody that confidence. Using all these courage tools will, too.

Remember your purpose

I use meditation as a gateway to writing. Each day I sit down, find my still center, and sink my roots into the earth. As I gather myself in, I connect with my higher self, and the words flow into and through me. Often I type with my eyes closed.

When you are ready to begin a new session of creative work, you will find it helpful to meditate or just sit in silence for a while. With your body still and your eyes closed, just allow yourself to settle into your body and bring your attention home from all of the places where it has wandered. Accept and allow whatever thoughts come, without worrying about them.

And as you sit quietly, remember the mission you are on, remember your *why*. I have my mission statements in their various forms posted on the white boards that surround my desk. If I look up from my meditation or my writing, I see the words that guide me.

Touching base with the reason you write is a powerful anchor. It helps you stay grounded in a sense of service, or mission, and not float around in your mind or your ego.

So spend some time communing with the purpose that you identified earlier in this book. Take the time to consider it, to allow the perfect words to float up. Take the time to write down your mission, either as a printed statement or a colorful handwritten note. Add illustrations. If the words come as a poem or a song, that works. Over time, this mission statement will evolve, until you settle on just the right sentence and it ceases to change. Then you'll know you've captured your purpose.

My personal mission statement took years to solidify. I began with asking the question, "What can I do to create additional streams of income?" and I progressed to asking, "What am I here to do? How can I serve?" and the answer came, and I recorded it, and later on I revised it, and finally I settled it. You know, all along I really wanted to go to a psychic and ask him or her to just tell me what I was here to do! I am impatient! But it doesn't work like that. Figuring out your purpose is part of your path, and it takes the time it takes.

Remembering your mission helps you deal with the dirt and the fear, because it reminds you of the reason the journey is worth walking.

Your creative journey has the power to heal you and help your readers, but it also holds tremendous healing for the planet itself. In fact, creativity is the most powerful tool I know for creating peace on earth.

Part Five: The Creative Path to a Healed Planet

Healing the planet is the journey of healing ourselves.
No more, no less.

It is not a coincidence that you are here on this planet at this time as a writer (or painter or artist or musician).

What happens when you create? You stand here on Earth and reach up and touch the heavens. And in this moment, you heal a small piece of yourself and an equal piece of the planet.

Just by touching god.

When we create, we *can* write from our minds: the surface, facile, clever, often unkind, part of ourselves, but when we are deep in the flow, some other energy guides our hand.

At the core of creativity is a connection with god. Your art is a gateway to god. Not the god of the bible, necessarily, although you can connect with him if you so choose, but the god of magic alive in the universe. Substitute *joy* or *peace* or *utter and complete happiness* for the word *god.* It's the same thing: the wondrous magic of the Source.

Each time we tap into source energy and anchor it in our words or images, we have aligned god with earth inside our own bodies. For that small moment, in that one place, the duality is healed and heaven does exist on earth. And as our art goes forth to touch the lives of others, the divine union spreads. Like dew, or mist. One day there will be enough, and the skies will open, and it will rain god.

You know the challenges facing our planet. You know that greed and arrogance challenge humanity's very existence. From famine to war to tumultuous weather, things are at a tipping point. Will we, as a people, move forward into our own divinity, or will we continue on the old path and escalate the destruction?

The world is at risk: Make art.

If all people for some significant portion of their day created art, whether through writing or painting or sculpting clay, planetary consciousness would evolve almost without our noticing. It is when the art is in us and we do not let it out that tension occurs. Illness is nothing but hearing the voice of the divine and telling it to come back later when we're less busy. Our creative force cannot be denied. When we do deny it, it leaves an emptiness behind. Don't be empty. Take time out of your day each day to sit in silence, and then, once you have heard the voice within, to honor that voice.

It matters so much how each one of us conducts our days. Our healing is not something that other people do for us while we are busy with our lives. Peace on earth is not a line item on someone else's budget, a job description for the favored few. No, it's my job and your job, too—the single most important thing any of us can do.

But you don't need to go work in soup kitchens or donate two years of your time to the Peace Corps. All you need to do, and all Spirit says you *must* do, is to carve out a significant portion of your day for the most significant thing you do—put your feet into the river of silence, plug into the divine, and *write.*

And then gather the words you were sent and release them to find their way in the world. Because, Writer, the world needs you. Earth needs the wisdom of all her children.

Part Six: The Journey Continues . . .

About Alix

My Spirit Says

My spirit says that I am
Here to be light, that I am
Here to be fearless,
Here to be an example.
My spirit says all is well.
My spirit says, teach peace,
Teach empowerment, teach the
Tools of living as a divine spark
Inside a human body.
Breathe.

Hi, I'm Alix.

I'm a writer, speaker, and teacher. I help writers connect with their creative spirits and transcend their fear so that they can create and market their writing with confidence and joy.

Life as a writer challenges us to grow into the people we were meant to be, but we don't have to do it the hard way.

We can use metaphysical tools that get us out of our minds and into our powerful, intuitive selves

It's my passion to support writers because I believe that creativity is a tremendously healing force for each of us individually, as well as for our planet and the collective consciousness.

When I'm not writing or presenting workshops, you can find me raising chickens, training cows, or napping on my organic farm, in Clarksburg, MD.

Books by Alix

The Abundance Diet for Writers
The Creative Flow Toolbox: *Holistic Solutions for Writer's Block*
Full Moon, New Earth: *Poems of Joy for the Collective Journey*
The Gift: *How My Horse Taught Me to Teach the Toughest Children*
Tapping the Well Within: *Writing from Your Source of Effortless Creativity, Deep Wisdom, and Utter Joy*
Writer, the World Needs You: *Get Past Your Fear and Write the Words You're Meant to Write*

Contact Alix

Email: alix@writerswithwings.com
Website: http://www.writerswithwings.com
Social media
    Twitter: @AuthorAlixMoore
    Facebook: WriterswithWings

Dear Reader,

Thank You!

I'm grateful that you've traveled with me through these pages. I hope these tools support your creative journey.

In case you haven't figured it out, it's my passion to help others connect with their powerful, peaceful, divinely creative selves.

I invite you to drop by my website, writerswithwings.com, and check out the resources I have gathered there to support your creativity.

I'd love to hear from you about how your creativity is blossoming or about the blocks you are overcoming. Please feel free to drop me an email at alix@writerswithwings.com.

In joy,

Alix

References

Agro, Christine,
    http://www.christineagro.com.

Allen, Robert G.
    2005, April. *Multiple streams of income.* Hoboken, NJ:
    Wiley.

Choquette, Sonia,
    http://soniachoquette.com.

————2005, June. *Trust your vibes: Secret tools for six-
    sensory living.* New York: Hay House, Inc.

Dyer, Wayne,
    http://www.drwaynedyer.com.

Goins, Jeff
    2012, April. *You are a writer (So start acting like one).*
    YourDigitalBook.com.

Grahl, Tim
    http://outthinkgroup.com

————2013, June. *Your first 1000 copies: The step-by-step guide to
    marketing your book.* Lynchburg, VA: Out:think Group.

Hay, Louise
    http://www.louisehay.com

Helmstetter, Shad
    2003, March. *Who are you really and what do you want?* Gulf
    Breeze, FL: Park Avenue Press.

19445848R00037

Made in the USA
Middletown, DE
21 April 2015